How to Protect Your Lifelong Savings (and Your Children's)

From the Costs of Long Term Care Should You Become Disabled

Keith Eliou, Esq.,CFP

How to Protect Your Lifelong Savings (and Your Children's) From the Costs of Long Term Care Should You Become Disabled

Printed by:CreateSpace Independent Publishing Platform

Copyright © 2017, Keith Eliou

Published in the United States of America

170731-00873-1

ISBN-13: 978-1978137578
ISBN-10: 1978137575

No parts of this publication may be reproduced without correct attribution to the author of this book.
For more information on 90-Minute Books including finding out how you can publish your own book, visit 90minutebooks.com or call (863) 318-0464

Here's What's Inside...

Part One

OVERVIEW OF PAYING FOR NURSING HOME CARE 1

A PLANNING EXAMPLE OF AN INDIVIDUAL ENTERING A NURSING HOME (A "CRISIS" SITUATION) 2

THE BASIC STEPS TO TAKE IN ORDER TO QUALIFY FOR MEDICAID TO PAY THE NURSING HOME AND TO PROTECT ASSETS IN THE CASE OF AN INDIVIDUAL 4

MARSHALL All Assets/Resources 5

Step One: Exclude Assets That Are Exempt 5

Step Two: Identify the Countable Assets/Resources 7

Step Three: Spend Down on Assets (When Appropriate) That May Be Excluded 8

Step Four: Calculate the Potential Savings Rate With the Basic Gift/Annuity Strategy 8

- **Step Five: How to Implement the Savings Strategy** 9
- **Step Six: What Happens to the Individual's Income?** 10
- **Step Seven: Revisit What Happens to the House Now That the Individual Is Living in the Nursing Home** 10
- **Step Eight: Review What Has Been Saved with the Above Strategy** 12

BE WARY OF THE UNCOMPENSATED TRANSFER PENALTY PITFALL? 13

THE OME RULE IN A SINGLE CASE 16

WHAT IF A FAMILY MEMBER DID WANT THE HOME, WHAT OPTIONS EXIST FOR REAL ESTATE? 18

OPTIONS FOR LIFE INSURANCE WITH A CASH VALUE OR TERM? 22

WHAT IF DENNIS OWNED A SINGLE FAMILY PROPERTY (VALUED AT $100,000 DOLLARS)THAT HE RENTED TO A TENANT? 24

WHAT IF DENNIS RECEIVED A $100,000 INHERITANCE AFTER HE BECAME ELIGIBLE AND BEGAN COLLECTING MEDICAID BENEFITS?... 25

WHAT IF DENNIS RECEIVED A $100,000 INHERITANCE AFTER HE WAS APPROVED FOR MEDICAID BUT WAS IN A PENALTY PERIOD AND PAYING THE NURSING HOME FROM HIS OWN PRIVATE FUNDS? 26

ADDITIONAL CONSIDERATIONS AFTER APPROVAL OF MEDICAID BENEFITS 27

WHAT TYPE OF PAPERWORK IS NEEDED TO PREPARE FOR A PUBLIC BENEFITS APPLICATION SUCH AS MEDICAID? 28

    CHECKLIST... 28

WHAT ARE THE IMPORTANT DATES AND THE TIMING OF THE MEDICAID APPLICATION PROCESS? 31

WHAT LEGAL DOCUMENTS SHOULD I HAVE PREPARED? 33

<u>Part Two</u>

MEDICAID PLANNING FOR A MARRIED COUPLE EXAMPLE... 37

STEP ONE: MARSHALL THE ASSETS............... 40

John and Mary Scenario with Income, Expenses, Assets and Liabilities 40

    Incomes... 40

    Housing Expenses........................ 40

    Assets... 41

    Life Insurance.. 41

STEP TWO: EXCLUDE ASSETS THAT ARE EXEMPT 42

STEP 3: SUBTRACT THE EXEMPT RESOURCES FROM THE TOTAL RESOURCES AND THAT BECOMES THE COUNTABLE RESOURCES.................................... 43

STEP 4: SUBTRACT THE RESOURCE ALLOWANCES FOR BOTH SPOUSES FROM THE COUNTABLE RESOURCES TO FIND EXCESS RESOURCES... 44

STEP 5: DETERMINE BEST WAY TO SPEND DOWN THE EXCESS RESOURCES........ 45

AT THE TIME OF THE APPLICATION FOR MEDICAID, HERE IS WHAT THE ASSETS WOULD LOOK LIKE ON FORM PA 600L: 47

WHAT IF JOHN AND MARY HAD DONE NOTHING TO PROTECT THEIR ASSETS? 49

PROTECTING "INCOME" OF THE COMMUNITY SPOUSE 50

Calculating The Income of the Community Spouse. 51

Step One: Add Income from the CSRA to Determine the Monthly Income 51

Step Two: Calculate If Mary Can Keep Over the Minimum Income Because of Shelter Costs 51

Step Three: Apply the Income First Rule to Shift Income to the Community Spouse 53

THE OME RULE IN A MARRIED CASE 55

ASSETS ACQUIRED AFTER MEDICAID APPROVAL 56

PRE-PLANNING OPTIONS TO PAY FOR LONG TERM CARE AND TO PROTECT ASSETS 57

The Irrevocable Trust............. 57

Long Term Care Insurance With Hybrid Policies 58

Disability Income Insurance 59

DISCLAIMER

This book is not intended to give legal advice and should not be relied upon by the reader for their particular situation. Generalizations have been made for the purpose of brevity. No two persons have the same combination of medical history, family relationships, type and amount of income and assets, all of which are critical in analyzing a scenario with the goal of arriving at potential strategies or solutions to meet their needs. You should not attempt to use the information in this book to execute strategies referenced herein on your own. The rules in this area can and do change frequently and the application of the rules can vary not only county by county but caseworker by caseworker. Furthermore, many of the rules only apply if certain conditions exist and often contain exceptions. The rules are a result of an interplay between federal and state statutes, case law, and regulations issued by the federal, state and county governments .Rather, consider the contents herein as potential options to consider with the sage advice of legal counsel.

HOW TO USE THIS BOOK

This book is focused on planning for or dealing with the process of becoming disabled, which most people will experience for at least a short period of time in their lives. This book is intended to provide the reader with information about current available options to pay for nursing home care, both before the need arises and during that time when immediate nursing home care becomes necessary.

Some statistics show that 70% of our population can expect to become disabled for a period of five years or more. With the growing cost of Medicaid draining federal and state funds, the author expects the future to include more difficulties regarding the qualifying process for Medicaid in paying for all of the costs of nursing home care. The reader should give great consideration in using this information, with a qualified professional, to pre-plan for the potential costs of at least five or more years in advance of the need.

Part One

OVERVIEW OF PAYING FOR NURSING HOME CARE

Now that the average cost of a stay in a nursing home has reached $10,000 or more per month, in less than three years, many couples can spend the amount it took a lifetime to accumulate on nursing home care. Some state governments are spending one out of every four dollars on these costs. Certainly, most government agencies will be considering ways to reduce that cost, including (but not limited to) making it more difficult to be eligible to obtain such public benefits.

The Medicaid rules and strategies will vary depending upon your status: marital, health, and financial. Variations will be based on whether you are an individual or a married couple, whether you are in good health or need assistance with two or more of the "activities of daily living" or ADLs (eating, bathing, dressing, toileting, continence, transferring from bed to chair), and which type and amount of assets you possess. Also, many states, including Pennsylvania, have "filial support" laws. Nursing homes rely on these laws to require children to pay the bill for their parents' care. To complicate strategies further, the Estate Recovery law enables the state to seek reimbursement once a person dies after receiving state-supported care.

A PLANNING EXAMPLE OF AN INDIVIDUAL ENTERING A NURSING HOME (A "CRISIS" SITUATION)

As stated above, the qualifications for the government to pay for your stay in a nursing home will vary depending upon your status as a single or married person. These are the two basic must-have rules for a single person to qualify for government-paid care: (1) a need for long-term care (i.e. generally requiring assistance with two or more ADLs) and (2) a financially destitute applicant. In the case of a married couple, certain financial protections are available for the healthy spouse who will continue to reside at home (called the "Community Spouse").

Let's look at the sample case of Dennis, a widower (single) at 70 years old who was just discharged from a hospital after a three-night qualified hospital stay (not observation status). He was sent to a nursing home for a period of rehabilitation. (It is very important to make certain the hospital stay is "qualified". Be aware of this issue, because if the stay is marked as "observation status" or it's not a qualified stay in some way, Medicare may not pay for the rehabilitation.) The rehabilitation component of Medicare will pay for the cost of care from 20 to 100 days (with some cost sharing) for days 21+

which may be paid for by a Medicare Advantage or Supplement Plan. Check with your insurance provider to find out if your cost-sharing portion is covered.

On day 21, the Medicare insurance provider says the health issue for which Dennis was treated has been resolved. He will be discharged to his home after two days. Medicare will not cover the need for long-term skilled care. He can appeal that decision by working his way through the appeals system. I can tell you from personal experience that this can take years to resolve. Let's further suppose Dennis can't get in and out of a bed by himself in order to dress, cook, or go to the bathroom. Failing to perform two or more of the ADLs may make him medically qualified for government-paid long-term skilled nursing home care, as long as Dennis can get a doctor to complete form MA-51 and have the local Area Agency on Aging ("AAA") confirm he is medically qualified.

However, if his income reaches more than $2,205 per month, the largest savings amount he is allowed equates to $2,400. If his monthly income is less than $2,205, he can keep $8,000 in total -savings (more details below). Assuming that his income is $2,000 per month, and that he has some significant assets (i.e. a house worth $150,000, a car worth $15,000, life insurance with a cash value of $5,000, and savings of $100,000), he won't qualify financially under Medicare. He will be faced with a bill of around

$300 per day to stay in the nursing home. Knowing he didn't plan ahead by purchasing long-term care insurance, and he doesn't want to drain his savings to pay the nursing home, what should he do?

THE BASIC STEPS TO TAKE IN ORDER TO QUALIFY FOR MEDICAID TO PAY THE NURSING HOME AND TO PROTECT ASSETS IN THE CASE OF AN INDIVIDUAL

Remember, you have to be medically and financially qualified. Other basic rules and qualifiers include the need to be a United States citizen, a resident of Pennsylvania (if you want Pennsylvania to pay for your care), and at the age of 65 or other categorical eligibility. Right now, this information is focused on the medical and financial aspects of qualifying for payment of services.

Again, to be medically qualified, Dennis needs a doctor to complete form MA-51 indicating that he is qualified as Nursing Facility Clinically Eligible (NFCE), and that he needs the AAA to complete their physical assessment and match the same diagnosis.

Second, he must also be Resource Eligible, meaning if his monthly income is $2,000, he can only have a maximum of $8,000 in savings.

Let's review his assets:

MARSHALL All Assets/ Resources

1. Home [valued at the lesser of the tax assessment, multiplied by the common level ratio or the appraised value] $150,000

2. Car [at Kelley *Blue Book*® value] $15,000

3. Life insurance [with a face value of $2,000, death benefit $25,000, and cash value] $5,000

4. Checking account $10,000

5. Mutual funds $240,000

6. IRA $50,000

TOTAL OF "ALL ASSETS/Resources"............................. $470,000

[GOAL: To Qualify for Medicaid, the "Countable Resources" must be less than $8,000 in this example]

Step One: Exclude Assets That Are Exempt

1. In Pennsylvania, the home is excluded from the initial qualifying calculation, but keep in mind two very important rules. First, when a person dies, the state can examine the value of the home for repayment of the costs for nursing home care. Second, with only $8,000 left in his accounts, Dennis may not be able to pay for the costs to maintain the home for expenses such as taxes, insurance, and utilities. Later, various real

estate strategies will be reviewed. You should consider these strategies if there is a child, sibling, or other family member who may have an interest in obtaining the house.

2. In addition to the house, $8,000 is also an amount excluded as the individual's resource allowance.

3. One car, regardless of the excluded value.

4. The first $1,000 of life insurance cash value is an excluded amount, assuming the face value of the policy is more than $1,500 (if less than $1,500, then all of the cash value is excluded).

5. Personal property and home furniture is typically excluded.

Step Two: Identify the Countable Assets/Resources

1. Life insurance—countable value is $5,000 less the $1,000 disregarded/exclusion amount.................. $4,000

(Note: Dennis may want to sell this policy if it is paid out to one of the children, because for the cost of the cash value, they can ultimately receive a $25,000 death benefit.)

2. Checking account $10,000

3. Mutual funds $240,000

4. IRA (gross value).................................... $50,000

(At this point, suppose that you will cash in this account and pay the income tax at a rate of 15% or $7,500, although the nursing home costs may provide for an offsetting medical deduction. Instead, you could draw the funds monthly, but then you would be seen as "over-resourced" and fail to qualify for Medicaid) IRA (net value)... $42,500

Countable ASSETS/Resources............ $296,500

LESS THE $8,000 RESOURCE ALLOWANCE PERMITTED

LEAVES TOTAL COUNTABLE Resources $288,500

Step Three: Spend Down on Assets (When Appropriate) That May Be Excluded

1. Purchase of a cemetery plot/monument; pay for opening and closing of grave $2,500

2. Pre-pay for funeral (amount limited by county) $11,500

4. Other spend-down options available on a case-by-case "if appropriate" basis: pay down debt, medical equipment, hearing aids, personal property (such as a television for the applicant's bedroom in the nursing home), home repairs, new roof or furnace (these amounts must be removed from the bank account in order to not be "available" and counted) $15,000

3. Attorney fees (ignored here for purposes of calculation, but deducted from countable assets) .... varies by case

TOTAL REMAINING COUNTABLE ASSETS **$259,500**

Step Four: Calculate the Potential Savings Rate with the Basic Gift/Annuity Strategy

1. Formula: Penalty divisor set by Pennsylvania for the cost of long-term care divided by [the Penalty Divisor + monthly nursing home medical costs less the monthly net income (gross less deductions for medical insurance premiums)]:

$9,792.65/$9,792.65 + $10,000 (estimated cost of all medical expenses including nursing home cost) − $1,750.10 ($2,000 gross minus $104.90

Medicare part B premium minus $145 (estimated cost for Medicare supplement premium) equals net income

Or $9,792.65/$9,792.65 + $10,000 − $1,750.10 = 54.27% saving rate

Essentially we should be able to save Dennis 54.27% of the $259,500 dollars or $140,830.

Step Five: How to Implement the Savings Strategy

1. Create an Irrevocable Trust ("Trust") and deposit into it $140,830 from the $259,500 dollars, thus protecting that amount from the cost of medical care, leaving the remainder of $118,669 to purchase a specific annuity which complies with the Deficit Reduction Act. This purchase will convert countable assets into a stream of income. As long as the monthly income of the annuity, combined with the other income of $1,750.10, is less than the cost of the monthly nursing home/medical care costs, Dennis will qualify for Medicaid. The transfer of the $140,830 to the trust will create a fifteen-month period of ineligibility for Medicaid ($140,830/$9,792.65 = $14.38). Now the $118,669 can be used to buy a fifteen-month annuity of $7,911.27 per month, combined with Dennis's net monthly income of $1,750.10, for $9,9661.37 per month. Remember the $10,000 nursing home/medical cost amount means that Dennis does not have enough to pay for the cost

of long-term care, since he has a shortfall of $38.63 a month for 15 months. His children, who are presumably the beneficiaries of the Trust, can make up the fifteen-month shortfall of $579.45.

Step Six: What Happens to the Individual's Income?

1. After the penalty expires, let's say Dennis qualifies for Medicaid. Minus allowances for his personal needs of $45 and the costs of any medical expenses, such as Medicare Part B and supplemental insurance premiums, his income will go to the nursing home as part of something called the Patient Pay Liability. Also, if he receives veteran benefits, Dennis can retain up to $90 per month.

Step Seven: Revisit What Happens to the House Now That the Individual Is Living in the Nursing Home

1. Remember that we excluded the house "for qualifying purposes". What happens now that Dennis only has $8,000 at his disposal to pay for taxes, insurance, utilities, and upkeep? Assuming that no one in the family is interested in keeping the house, although other options will be explored later, suppose the house is sold for $150,000. Within 10 days, Dennis will be obliged to report the sale and receipt of proceeds to the

County Assistance Office ("the County"), at which time he will be termed "over-resourced" and ineligible for Medicaid, i.e. he'll get kicked off the program. One option or solution would be to take about half of the money and put it into the Trust, using the other half to buy another annuity to pay through the penalty period created with that transfer, termed an "uncompensated transfer".

Step Eight: Review What Has Been Saved With the Above Strategy

1. **If Dennis had done nothing,** he would have either paid the nursing home directly or paid the State indirectly:

- (a) The value of the home $150,000
- (b) The cash value of life insurance (i.e. losing the $25,000 death benefit) $5,000
- (c) The checking account $10,000
- (d) Mutual funds $240,000
- (e) IRA principal (generally $50,000) of conservative AFTER-TAX VALUE $42,500

A TOTAL OF $447,500

Personal assets (i.e. the car, furniture, and personal property) are not listed here because they are exempt items; theoretically, as exempt items, Dennis could give them to his children.

2. Amount we managed to save:

- (a) Half the value of the house $75,000
- (b) Assets transferred into the Trust $140,830
- (c) Cost of funeral and burial, cemetery plots, etc ($2,500 + $11,000) $13,500
- (d) Home improvements, medical equipment, personal property $15,000

TOTAL AMOUNT SAVED $244,330

BE WARY OF THE UNCOMPENSATED TRANSFER PENALTY PITFALL

One of the federal government's rules basically says that if you "give away" any of your money in the five years prior to the date you applied for Medicaid (the "open date"), you will be ineligible for the benefit of the government paying for your care for a certain period of time. The period of time is determined by dividing the total amount of gifts by $321.95, and rounding down to the nearest day. That amount is the current daily "penalty divisor" (the monthly amount is $9,792.65). Many people are surprised by the government's definition of "giving away your money". If you give Christmas presents, donate to a church, pay for your grandchildren's tuition costs or weddings, those payments are all marked as "gifts" and can result in a penalty period, during which you are ineligible for Medicaid to pay for your nursing home stay.

Let's suppose that over the previous five years, Dennis made checks payable to "CASH" of $600 a month for spending money and groceries. Also, he paid his daughter $600 a month for helping him around the house. That's $1,200 multiplied by 60 months (5 years) for a total of $72,000. The bad news is that those transfers would most likely be termed "uncompensated" and mean he would be penalized for about 7.35 months, while remaining ineligible for Medicaid to pay the nursing home. Therefore, the amount protected above would probably be REDUCED by about $72,000. If there are not enough funds to pay the nursing home, then the children could be sued under the filial support laws to pay the nursing home. The good news is Dennis can (mostly) avoid this problem rather easily. You are probably thinking, "Wait a minute, he didn't gift anything." However, the government presumes (absent proof to the contrary) any transfers for cash—including cash withdrawals—to be "uncompensated" (i.e. a gift), so the money given to his daughter would be treated as a gift because it is presumed that she helped him out of love and affection.

As an alternative, he could have paid for his groceries with a check payable to the supermarket or via a credit card which would have shown the store as the payee. As for his daughter, either he could have given her $500 a month (and not a penny more). As long as he didn't make any other unaccounted-for transfers in any single month, that $500 would not be counted as an uncompensated transfer. It would not result in a penalty. Keep in mind, if he gave her $500 and then gave someone else $10 that he couldn't account for, the entire $510 could be penalized, not just the $10 over the $500.

The other option for Dennis is to elect for his daughter to enter into a written **Caregiver Agreement**. The catch is that he would have had to do this *prior to* giving any money to his daughter, not after. The agreement would need to specify the services that the daughter was to perform, and the payments would need to be commensurate with what he would pay for the services on the open market. His daughter should also report the payment on her tax return, and income and payroll taxes should have been paid. As a caution, Dennis should not try to draft this type of contract on his own, but rather seek the advice of a qualified attorney.

As briefly mentioned above, a potentially worse problem could arise if Dennis decided not to seek the help of an experienced attorney, and just paid for his nursing home stay with his own money until it was gone. If Dennis did that and then applied for Medicaid to pay for his care, he would have been told he was ineligible until he paid for the first 7.35 months and would be required to privately pay the nursing home. In many cases, the private cost of care is more than the government monthly divisor of $9,792.65, so the amount could be more than the $72,000. Since he would have been broke, most likely the care facility would expect his children to disburse that payment. If they didn't pay voluntarily, then the nursing home would most likely file a lawsuit. Also, the nursing home might look at discharging Dennis.

THE OME RULE IN A SINGLE CASE

There is a rule which sometimes applies in these situations, in which the nursing home resident can use part of their current Patient Pay Liability, which would otherwise pay the nursing home for the "current month", to actually pay for "prior months" when they stayed in the home, before they were approved for payment through Medicaid.

For example, suppose Dennis entered a nursing home on May 1, 2017, and today is June 13, 2017. Dennis has $18,000 in the bank and has already paid for a funeral and burial—items which can achieve retroactive approval although retroactivity is not available in this example. However, Dennis also has $10,000 of credit card debt and his income is low enough to qualify for the Resource Allowance at $8,000. Dennis pays off the $10,000 and, assuming he is medically qualified since he is staying in the nursing home, he is eligible for Medicaid on June 13. But he still owes the home for May 1 through June 13. If these bills are not paid, the home could pursue Dennis's children. However, since there was no gifting in this case, Dennis could request that his income, which would otherwise go to the nursing home as Patient Pay for the current month of June, should be directed first to the prior billing for May 1 through June 13. Of course, if Dennis dies before that time frame is paid, his children could still be pursued for payment. Dennis should also have his checking account with the $8,000 placed in joint names with the right of survivorship stated, so that if he passes away, that amount would not be part of the probate estate. Thus, it would not be subject to estate recovery to pay for his stay in the nursing home.

WHAT IF A FAMILY MEMBER DID WANT THE HOME, WHAT OPTIONS EXIST FOR REAL ESTATE?

1. Let's suppose that one of his children lived (as a caretaker) with Dennis for at least the past two years, and "but for" that care taken, he would have needed to be in a nursing home. If the caretaker owns no other home, and if a doctor will verify that their care enabled him to stay at home, then Dennis could transfer the home to that caretaker without a penalty. The child would take the father's basis but that may not be an issue if they lived there two out of the next five years. This would also be true if Dennis had a "special needs" child or a trust for that special needs child, regardless of whether that child lived with him or helped Dennis as a caregiver. By the way, the above exemption can be used in conjunction with a Caregiver Agreement to pay a child for help before Dennis needs nursing home care.

2. Next, assume that Dennis is in a nursing home (a crisis situation). He has a child who doesn't meet the above Child Caregiver exemption but who wants to buy his home. There are several different options to consider.

   (a) Dennis could sell his entire home for half the value to one of his children. (Note: there is a potential basis issue for the purposes of capital tax gain.) The child's basis is what the child paid (i.e. half the value), so if the child sells the property, he or she may be subject to a capital gains tax for the difference between the sales price and what he or she paid. However, if the child lives in that home as a principal residence for two of the next five years, then the child may not be subject to that tax. If Dennis died within one year of the transfer, then the child might be subject to the payment of inheritance tax on the half gifted. As for Dennis, the gift of half of the equity in the house would count as a penalty for Medicaid purposes. Most likely, he would be best served if he used the proceeds from the sale to buy a qualified annuity to pay through the penalty period.

(b) Dennis could sell HALF of his home to one of the children and retain HALF with the right of survivorship, without making a gift. If he doesn't engage in another strategy, he would have additional resources to potentially use to pay the nursing home. On the pro side, his child just potentially received the house for half the price and would get a step up in basis on the other half at dad's death. Inheritance tax would be due in this case, not capital gains tax, and there would be no estate recovery. The other half of the house would pass to the child by operation of law and not through the probate estate. On the con side, the house should not be sold before Dennis dies, or his share could present a problem for Medicaid eligibility. The same could result if the child dies before Dennis.

(c) Retain a life estate in his home and transfer the remainder interest to his children. The value of the interest transferred would create a penalty period for the children's father. They may find, depending on Dad's age at the time of the transfer, that most of the value would still be allocated to his interest. This often presents challenges in other areas, for example, in obtaining a mortgage on the property. On the pro side, if Dennis dies first, the home passes outside of his probate estate although inheritance tax would be due on the whole amount.

(d) Sell the home and use the proceeds to buy a life estate in the home of one of his children. If Dennis lived there for at least one year, then this would not be a penalized transfer. Again, while Dennis is alive, obtaining a mortgage on this type of split-interest real estate is problematic. Upon dad's death, the kids may have to pay inheritance tax on the whole amount. If both children die first, then their remainder interest may go to a third party.

(e) If a sibling is listed as one of the owners of the father's current home, and has lived there for at least a year prior to entrance into a nursing home, the home could be transferred to that sibling without a penalty.

OPTIONS FOR LIFE INSURANCE WITH A CASH VALUE OR TERM

1. It may be possible to sell a term policy to a third-party company if the policy has a significant death benefit ($50,000 or more). Typically, companies don't want to get involved with smaller policies. This strategy can also work with a term policy, if you no longer wish to make the payments but would like to receive some value for what you have paid over the life of the policy.

2. Special rules apply, for Medicaid purposes, to insurance policies with an aggregate face value of $1,500 or more per person. (The face value is the amount for which the policy was initially issued.) Cash value builds up as premiums are paid (except for term insurance) and the Death Benefit is the amount that the beneficiary will be paid upon the death of the insured. Some policies have a much greater cash value than face value. If the aggregate face values of all of the policies total $1,500 or less, then none of the cash value is counted as a resource for Medicaid purposes. (As a side note, some of these policies are tied to associated stock, which counts as an available asset.) If they have face values in excess of $1,500 then the first $1,000 of cash value is exempt, and the rest counts as an available resource.

One option to consider, when planning for Medicaid, is whether it makes sense to transfer the ownership, cash value, and death benefit of a paid-up policy to a funeral home as pre-payment for a funeral. The cost of the funeral cannot be "excessive" as determined by the County Assistance Office in Pennsylvania (again, "the County"). For example, if you have a paid-up whole life policy with a cash value of $5,000 and a Death Benefit of $10,000, theoretically, you could assign that policy to the funeral home as payment, thereby reducing your available resources by $5,000 but actually leveraging the transfer and getting a $10,000 benefit. Most likely, a local funeral home can offer more information on this topic.

Another option was mentioned in the earlier Individual scenario. If the death benefit is far in excess of the cash value, and it's a paid-up policy, a parent could potentially gift the policy to one of his (or her) children and incur a penalty for the transfer, but he would get a Death Benefit far in excess of the penalized amount. For example, if the cash value was $5,000 but the Death Benefit was $25,000, then making the gift might make sense.

WHAT IF DENNIS OWNED A SINGLE FAMILY PROPERTY (VALUED AT $100,000 DOLLARS) THAT HE RENTED TO A TENANT?

Most likely the real estate would be viewed as "exempt" (as an essential part of self-support), but the collected rent would go toward his Patient Pay balance at the nursing home. This could be an issue, since the rent would not be available to pay any mortgage or expenses on the property. Dennis might be able to set up the lease so that the tenant would pay the expenses directly to the mortgage holder, as well as paying the taxes and insurance directly to the collector and insurance agency. The best solution might be to sell the property, and then (potentially) protect some of the proceeds by engaging in planning.

WHAT IF DENNIS RECEIVED A $100,000 INHERITANCE AFTER HE BECAME ELIGIBLE AND BEGAN COLLECTING MEDICAID BENEFITS?

He would have to report the receipt of such funds within 10 days to the County. At which time, without planning, he would be marked as "over-resourced" and ineligible for benefits. He might be able to engage in "half-a-loaf gifting" in which he would basically gift $50,000 to a trust, and buy a Medicaid Compliant Qualified Annuity to privately pay the nursing home through the penalty period associated with the gift. This is a high-level overview and not to be taken literally as half, because the penalty divisor is not $10,000 exactly.

WHAT IF DENNIS RECEIVED A $100,000 INHERITANCE AFTER HE WAS APPROVED FOR MEDICAID BUT WAS IN A PENALTY PERIOD AND PAYING THE NURSING HOME FROM HIS OWN PRIVATE FUNDS?

Dennis could use the funds to help to pay the nursing home privately during the penalty period. He could spend it on items for personal use and replenish his $8,000 resource allowance. If he gifted it, that would result in a further penalty. If he had funds left over after the penalty period, that situation could result in excess resources which could prevent him from qualifying for Medicaid immediately. At that point, he could contact the Department of Human Services, a third-party liability department for estate recovery, and pre-pay the additional resources to that department to offset future liability for Medicaid payments made on his behalf. He could also engage in additional planning by gifting part of the excess funds to a trust and buying another Medicaid Compliant Qualified Annuity to pay through the additional penalty period.

ADDITIONAL CONSIDERATIONS AFTER APPROVAL OF MEDICAID BENEFITS

Dennis should avoid acquiring assets in his name alone because they would be part of what Pennsylvania calls his Probate Estate (i.e. items in his name alone that won't pass by operation of law or beneficiary designation). This could result in making him "over-resourced" with too many assets and thus ineligible for Medicaid.

Presumably, once he is qualified to receive Medicaid, all of his assets are now in the Trust. However, he would probably want to name one of his children to fill the "In trust for" slot on his checking account so that any funds in that account will not pass by probate, although inheritance tax will still be due.

If Dennis became the beneficiary of another person's assets (through a will, trust, life insurance policy, etc.), a third-party trust with Dennis as the beneficiary could be created. This trust could be named as the beneficiary, so that any funds received would go directly to the trust (not outright to Dennis), and so should not cause a problem for his Medicaid eligibility or remove Dennis as the beneficiary altogether. Possibly, his children could be substituted for Dennis.

WHAT TYPE OF PAPERWORK IS NEEDED TO PREPARE FOR A PUBLIC BENEFITS APPLICATION SUCH AS MEDICAID?

The documentation is intense. Think about this: you are asking the government to pick up hundreds of thousands of dollars for your costs. Be prepared to show them you qualify for this huge benefit

CHECKLIST
1. Photo ID for the applicant and spouse.

2. Photo ID for the agent under a Power of Attorney and the Power of Attorney paperwork.

3. Social Security Card for the applicant and spouse.

4. Birth Certificate for the applicant and spouse.

5. Military paperwork (Honorable Discharge, separation papers, etc.)

6. Naturalization papers or alien/refugee registration cards for applicant and spouse.

7. Marriage, divorce, and/or death certificate for applicant and spouse.

8. Medicare card and supplement health insurance cards for applicant and spouse (front and back).

9. Private health insurance and/or prescription plan premium invoices for the applicant and spouse.

10. Nursing home bills and any unpaid medical bills from the past three months.

11. Proof of resources owned solely or jointly by the applicant, such as, but not limited to these:

   a) Checking or savings account (most current statement needed)
   b) Hospitalization or accident insurance policies
   c) Statement of cash on hand
   d) Prepaid funeral and burial arrangements, burial plots, etc.
   e) Stocks or bonds
   f) Credit union accounts
   g) Trust funds
   h) Life insurance policies, as well as verification of current face value, cash and death values. Also, beneficiary designations of policies
   i) IRAs or other retirement accounts
   j) Certificates of Deposits
   k) Mutual Funds
   l) Annuities

12. Bank statements, all pages, for the past 60 months, as well as proof of any accounts closed in the past 60 months.

13. Proof of all income received by the applicant and spouse, such as (but not limited to) the following:

   a) Social security award letter
   b) Union benefits
   c) Black Lung
   d) Pensions
   e) Veterans benefits
   f) Railroad retirements

14. Income tax returns, W2s, and 1099s for the past five years. NOTE: Even if your income doesn't rise to the level of the need to file federal tax returns, you should file, so the application will not be delayed because you don't provide these documents.

15. Verification of housing costs for a spouse living at home, such as (but not limited to) the following:

   a) Rent/Mortgage
   b) Utility costs (Water, Sewage, Gas, Electric, Phone, Trash)
   c) Insurance
   d) Property taxes
   e) Homeowners' dues

16. Title, registration and insurance for any motor vehicles, mobile homes owned by the applicant and/or spouse.

17. Any forms completed upon admission to a nursing home, including but not limited to the "Resource Assessment" (PA 1572).

WHAT ARE THE IMPORTANT DATES AND THE TIMING OF THE MEDICAID APPLICATION PROCESS?

Remember, to be approved for Medicaid, you must be marked as "otherwise eligible", meaning that you meet both the medical requirement of being NFCE (Nursing Facility Clinically Eligible) and the financial requirement of having assets under the applicable resource limit of $2,400 or $8,000.

Let's assume that you met the Medicaid requirements on March 1, 2017. You were in a nursing home on that date and under the resource limit. Today is June 20, 2017. You file the application with the County and ask for benefits starting on March 1, the day you were otherwise eligible (called the "open date"). You can request benefits beginning on the first day of the third month prior to the month you apply. The County has 45 business days to review your application. Once your application is reviewed, the caseworker will review your financial statements for the five years prior to June 20 and do a "lookback" review for uncompensated transfers. If any are found, and if your application is approved, most likely the caseworker will assess a penalty in which you will be ineligible for benefits from the "open date" forward, according to the daily penalty divisor. This 45-day process can be extended if the caseworker has questions, in which case you may receive a denial with the opportunity to submit additional information and to attend a mediation. If you are still denied benefits, you may request a "Fair Hearing" with an Administrative Law Judge.

For a married couple, when the caseworker is reviewing the financial qualifications, she will look at the date you were admitted to a nursing facility for a period of 30 or more days. Next, she will review the Resource Assessment for the purpose of determining the Community Spouse Resource Allowance.

WHAT LEGAL DOCUMENTS SHOULD I HAVE PREPARED?

1. A properly drafted Power of Attorney ("POA"). This is a crucial document. If you wait until you are disabled, you may not have the capacity to legally execute this document. In the POA you (as the Principal) give another person (your Agent) the power to take certain actions on your behalf, some of which could be essential for engaging in effective Medicaid planning. Certain "hot powers" are required to be specified in the POA in order for your Agent to have the authority to undertake them. In many cases, POAs should be drafted with the idea of giving expansive powers to the Agent for Medicaid Planning.

2. Create a will. In the case of an individual, name an Executor in the event that you own property or have received property which must pass by or under a will (through probate). Keep in mind, if you structure your assets properly when planning for Medicaid eligibility, you should not have an estate to pass through probate. If you do, it will be subject to estate recovery and lost. In the case of a married person, the will of the healthy community spouse should be amended to reduce the amount given to the institutionalized spouse to approximately one-third. The other two-thirds should pass to other beneficiaries such as children (or possibly a trust for the benefit of the institutionalized spouse). If the community spouse dies before the

institutionalized spouse, the bulk of the estate will be sheltered from the long-term care cost of the institutionalized spouse.

3. Draft a Health Care Power of Attorney and Living Will. In the Health Care Power of Attorney ("HCPOA"), you give another person power to make decisions about your medical care (as opposed to financial decisions) in the event of your incapacity. In the Living Will, you make decisions about what you would like to be done with respect to end-of-life decision making.

4. Potentially draft a Revocable Trust. While this does not protect your assets from creditors, it can be useful to name as a beneficiary of other assets or life insurance. Rather than changing beneficiary designations on many different instruments (such as bank/brokerage accounts, real estate, insurance, etc.), all of the assets could name this Trust, and then you could just make changes to the Trust if you want to reallocate who receives the benefits. This is also widely used in cases where you would own real estate in another state in order to avoid what is known as "ancillary administration". Single individuals, without someone who could act as an agent under a POA, sometimes use this vehicle and name a bank or corporate trustee to manage the Trust assets. A trustee, unlike an agent under a POA, has relatively liberal powers unless otherwise restrained by the Principal who creates the Trust.

5. Potentially draft an Irrevocable Trust. This can have the effect of protecting assets. The person who creates this Trust (the Settlor) can retain some controls, but care should be taken because retaining too much or the wrong type of control could result in the loss of asset protection. In some cases, the principal residence is an asset which can be placed in the Trust. If properly prepared, the Grantor may still reside in the property and retain the federal capital gains tax exclusion, while the beneficiaries can take advantage of a step up in basis.

6. Create a Caregiver Agreement. This is often used in pre-planning for Medicaid benefits. As mentioned earlier, parents sometimes give their children money for helping them but, absent a written agreement specifying the future services to be provided (not past services) and payments commensurate with what would be paid in the open market, any money paid would mostly likely viewed as a "gift" by the parents and create a period of ineligibility for Medicaid.

7. Draft a deed for the transfer of the primary residence to an exempt beneficiary, such as under the Child Caregiver exemption. This is an exemption for a child, not a grandchild or other caregiver. Under certain conditions, including the child residing in the house for the past two years and "but for" the help of the child, the parent would have needed nursing home care, the home can be transferred without penalty to that child.

8. Possibly draft a Special Needs Trusts. These are created to benefit a person with special needs and to keep that person from losing any public benefits they are receiving.

Part Two

MEDICAID PLANNING FOR A MARRIED COUPLE EXAMPLE

Planning for a married couple is different than planning for an individual. In the case of a married couple, if one of them needs long-term skilled care, rules exist to protect the Community Spouse who will continue to live at home, from losing all of their assets and income to the cost of care for the Institutionalized Spouse in the nursing home. On the date the spouse enters a nursing home, they should fill out a Resource Assessment Form from which is calculated the Community Spouse Resource Allowance ["CSRA"]. The CSRA allows the spouse at home to basically keep half of the assets subject to a minimum amount (currently $24,180) and a maximum amount (currently $120,900). This allowance is part of anti-impoverishment rules set by the government to protect the Community Spouse.

The Community Spouse can also keep a certain amount of income subject to a minimum amount (currently $2,030 per month) and a maximum amount (currently $3,022.50 per month). In some cases, the Community Spouse can shift income from the Institutionalized Spouse or keep additional income-generating assets to meet the minimum income permitted. If the Community Spouse has costs termed "excess shelter costs", which can result from high medical expenses such as costs for an assisted care facility, or if the Community Spouse has very low monthly income, he (or she) may be able to keep more than the minimum income up to the maximum amount allowed (more than the maximum would require an appeal to a fair hearing). There may also be the opportunity for Veterans Benefits for those with high medical expenses, but that topic will be left for another book.

In calculating financial eligibility of the Institutionalized Spouse for Medicaid, the first step is to categorize the resources into what is inaccessible (not under the control of the applicant, perhaps gifts which could create a penalty), what is exempt (or possibly "Unavailable"), and what is countable.

Exempt resources can include personal effects: a principal residence up to a certain amount of equity (assuming an intent to return by the Institutionalized Spouse); one automobile; certain types of life insurance; cemetery plots and irrevocable funeral and burial reserves; resource allowances for both the Community Spouse and Institutionalized Spouse; real or personal property used in a trade or business essential for self-support; and the Community Spouse's retirement account.

Unavailable assets may include the equity in a vacation home. The County will require it to be made available, if possible, so it will have to be dealt with at some point. For purposes of the initial application of Medicaid, the equity would not be considered a Countable Resource.

To be eligible, the Institutionalized Spouse can have Countable Resources of no more than $2,400 unless their current gross income is below $2,205—then they can keep $8,000. One strategy is to convert into exempt status those assets which would otherwise be Countable Resources, but the timing of the conversion is important because it can impact the calculations for the amount which can be retained by the Community Spouse under their CSRA or Resource allowance.

One exempt resource is the CSRA. As previously mentioned, this is the amount of assets the Community Spouse can keep. The Resource Assessment is given to the applicant when she enters the Nursing Home with the Admissions Notice Packet (MA 401) from the Department of Human Services ("DHA"). On this form, all the assets of the applicant and/or spouse are listed. The date of the form becomes known as the "snapshot date", assuming a stay of at least 30 consecutive days in a long-term care facility. As mentioned earlier, the Community Spouse can keep half of the assets/resources as of that date, subject to a minimum and maximum set amount. The DHS will calculate this number, but an experienced attorney should perform the calculation as well to make certain the County's figures are correct.

STEP ONE: MARSHALL THE ASSETS

John and Mary Scenario with Income, Expenses, Assets and Liabilities

John has just entered a Nursing Home. His age is 79 and Mary's age is 76. These numbers represent their incomes, expenses, assets and liabilities.

Incomes

John:

Social Security per month (gross) $1,400

Pension per month (gross) $500

Mary:

Social Security per month (gross) $1,000

Housing Expenses

Condo Fee per month $500

Mortgage payment per month $400

Homeowners insurance $100

Total $1000

Electric bill, not including heat $125/month

Telephone $75/month

Assets

Condo worth $200,000 with a $20,000 mortgage

Household furnishings and personal property $20,000

Car (five years old) .... value $10,000

John's IRA $50,000

Mary's IRA $75,000

Five cemetery plots for John and Mary and their children ... $1,000 each

Joint Checking $25,000

Joint Savings $125,000

Joint CD $30,000

Life Insurance

John:

Policy 1: Face Value of $2,000, Cash Value of $5,000, and Death Benefit of $6,000

Policy 2: Term insurance policy with Face Value of $4,000, $0 cash value

Mary:

Policy 3: Face Value of $11,000, Cash Value of $8,000, and Death Benefit of $8,000

Policy 4: Face Value of $7,000 and Cash Value of $500

STEP TWO: EXCLUDE ASSETS THAT ARE EXEMPT

1. The Condo is a personal residence in which the Community Spouse (Mary) will live. It is exempt. Most likely, she will want to transfer the ownership into her name alone, prior to filing a Medicaid application. Provided that Mary's will gets updated, this will most likely protect the home for the benefit of their kids, and from John's long-term care costs if Mary sells the home or dies before John.

2. Household Furnishings and personal effects are usually exempt. This might not hold true if these consisted of valuable works of art.

3. One car is always exempt.

4. The IRA/retirement account of the Community Spouse (Mary) is exempt. However, John's IRA is a Countable Resource.

5. Cemetery Plots, even for the whole family, are typically exempt.

6. The first $1,000 of cash value of life insurance policies are usually exempt, possibly more if the aggregate face value for each spouse is less than $1,500. All term and group policies are exempt.

STEP 3: SUBTRACT THE EXEMPT RESOURCES FROM THE TOTAL RESOURCES AND THAT BECOMES THE COUNTABLE RESOURCES

John's IRA $50,000

The joint checking account, savings
account, and CD $180,000

John's excess cash value of life
insurance ($5,000 – $1,000) $4,000

Mary's excess cash value of life
insurance ($8,000 + 500 – $1,000) $7,500

Total Countable resources on
admission date to Nursing home.......... **$241,500**

STEP 4: SUBTRACT THE RESOURCE ALLOWANCES FOR BOTH SPOUSES FROM THE COUNTABLE RESOURCES TO FIND EXCESS RESOURCES

Mary is permitted to keep as her CSRA half <u>up to</u> $120,900 .... she keeps $120,750

John, based upon his income of less than $2,205 per month, is permitted to keep $8,000

This example means that John and Mary have **Excess Resources** that will prevent John from having Medicaid pay for his nursing home stay of **$112,750**

STEP 5: DETERMINE BEST WAY TO SPEND DOWN THE EXCESS RESOURCES

Determine the best way to spend the excess resources of $112,750 in order to qualify for Medicaid

1. The $20,000 mortgage could be paid off, thus reducing the excess to $92,750.

2. Mary's life insurance policy (with a face value of $11,000, cash value of $8,000, and death benefit of $8,000) could be used to pay part of her funeral home expenses by naming the funeral home as owner and beneficiary. Another $2,000 could be used to pay the difference, assuming the cost is $10,000, so that reduces the excess to $82,750.

3. Do the same with John's life insurance policy (with a $2,000 face value and $5,000 cash value): transfer ownership, change the beneficiary designation to the funeral home, plus pay an additional $5,000 (for a total of $10,000). Thereby, the excess would be reduced to $72,750.

4. Pay for the burial expenses of grave opening and closing and monument of $2,750, bringing the excess to $70,000.

5. Mary could trade in the older car and pay $20,000 in cash toward a new car, leaving the excess amount at $50,000.

6. John's IRA could be cashed in and the tax paid, assuming a 20% rate of $10,000, leaving the excess at $40,000.

7. It's either possible to pay for home improvements (be careful—the money must be paid to the contractor to avoid it being counted—as long as John or Mary have the money, it counts as a resource) or buy a Single Premium Immediate Annuity for Mary's benefit. This annuity must be Medicaid-compliant in order to provide her with additional income.

AT THE TIME OF THE APPLICATION FOR MEDICAID, HERE IS WHAT THE ASSETS WOULD LOOK LIKE ON FORM PA 600L:

1. Mary would own the Condo outright ($200,000);

2. The household furnishings and personal property would be protected $20,000;

3. Mary would have a new car owned free and clear ($30,000);

4. John would have $0 in his IRA;

5. Mary would have her IRA valued at $75,000;

6. All five cemetery plots would be protected ($1,000 each);

7. The pre-arranged funeral for both John and Mary would be paid ($20,000);

8. The grave openings, closings, and monuments would be paid ($2,750);

9. John's term insurance policy would be exempt ($4,000);

10. Mary's cash value of life insurance would be exempt ($500);

11. Mary's CSRA would be exempt ($120,750);

12. John's Institutionalized Spouse Resource Allowance would be exempt ($8,000);

13. If Mary elected for a Single Premium Immediate Annuity ("SPIA"), it would be exempt ($40,000)

(Note: If she didn't elect the SPIA, there may be other options which might allow her to increase her income or protect more assets.)

WHAT IF JOHN AND MARY HAD DONE NOTHING TO PROTECT THEIR ASSETS?

At a minimum, the immediate at-risk assets are the excess resources of $112,750. There are potential assets at risk of being consumed by the costs of John's nursing home care, in the event that Mary dies before John, so as much as $496,500 could be at risk for the cost of John's nursing home care.

1. The condo worth $200,000 with a $20,000 mortgage, net equity $180,000

2. John's IRA $50,000

3. The joint checking account, savings account, and CD $180,000

4. The cash values of life insurance at risk $11,500

5. Mary's IRA $75,000

Total that would have been spent on nursing home care $496,500

If Mary dies before John, without additional planning (i.e. a community spouse will and deed and the change of beneficiary designations), John would inherit all of the assets. He would be deemed ineligible for Medicaid, and otherwise forced to pay for his care until he established eligibility.

PROTECTING "INCOME" OF THE COMMUNITY SPOUSE

Mary is permitted to keep income subject to a minimum amount (currently $2,030 per month) and a maximum amount ($3,022.50).

In this scenario, Mary receives $1,000 per month from Social Security.

Let's assume that Mary didn't purchase a SPIA for now. If she did, and if the monthly SPIA payment along with her $1,000 from Social Security pushed her over the $2,030 per month minimum, generally, she would not be able to keep other sources of income or assets.

CALCULATING INCOME FOR MARY, THE COMMUNITY SPOUSE

Step One: Add Income Generated From the CSRA to Determine the Monthly Income

In addition to Mary's benefit of $1,000 per month from Social Security, the County will assume that Mary's CSRA ($120,750) can generate 1.5%, or $150.94 per month, or $1,811.25 per year.

Therefore, Mary's income, for calculation of what she can keep, would be $1,150.94.

Again, she can keep between $2,030 and $3,022.50 per month. To calculate if she can keep more than the $2,030 minimum amount, the County would look for excess shelter costs.

Step Two: Calculate If Mary Can Keep Over the Minimum Income Because Of Shelter Costs

Shelter costs are for expenses such as mortgage payments, real estate taxes, homeowners' insurance, condominium fees, rent, assisted living facility fees, or personal care home fees. The standard Shelter Cost amount is currently $609.

Utility bills are also taken into account and certain allowances are made. For example, the Standard Heating Allowance is $570, Non-heating is $296, and Phone Allowance is $33.

In certain instances when the applicant is expected to return home within six months, there is a potential Home Maintenance Deduction of $757.10 with a six-month limit. This rule would not apply in this scenario because we are assuming the doctor indicated on the MA 51 that John's stay would be more than six months.

In this instance, the current monthly housing expenses are $1,000.

In the Condo, Mary does not have to pay for heat, and her electric and phone bill together cost $200 per month, so we would use the Standard Allowance of $296 (since it is higher than the actual amount). The total shelter costs, including utilities, would be $1,296; then the Standard Shelter cost of $609 would be subtracted, so John and Mary are left with Excess Shelter Costs of $687. Add the $687 to the Minimum Income Permitted amount of $2,030, and we find that Mary may keep $2,717 per month for income. If the amount were more than the Maximum Income Permitted amount of $3,022.50, then Mary would have to go through a Fair Hearing process involving an Administrative Law Judge, in order to keep more than the maximum.

To recap, Mary is permitted to keep $2,717 per month; she has a Social Security allocation of $1,000 per month. The County assumes she has income from the CSRA of $150.94 per month. The difference of $1566.06 comes first from John's income, as the Institutionalized Spouse.

Step Three: Apply the Income First Rule to Shift Income to the Community Spouse

John's income from Social Security and his pension total $1,900 per month. He is permitted to keep $45 as a personal needs allowance and his Medicare Part B premium of $140.90 and his Medigap premium of $100 (an assumed amount), which leaves him $1,614.10 as an amount available for Mary. She would get the $1,566.06 while the remainder would be sent to the nursing home as John's Patient Pay Liability toward the monthly bill.

If John's income was insufficient to make up the difference for what Mary could keep, she could keep additional resources which would generate income sufficient to bring her up to her minimum income allowance ($2,717). As a practical matter, you may be required to obtain three quotes from annuity providers to show the amount of assets needed to generate the shortfall in Mary's income.

Of course, while this is a very good result for Mary and permits her to live with greater income, should John pass away, that income stream would come to an end. Mary could apply to the Social Security Administration for an increase based upon John's history.

THE OME RULE IN A MARRIED CASE

Earlier, we discussed how the patient in a nursing home can have a portion of their "current" Patient Pay income directed to pay the cost of the nursing home (and any other medical expenses incurred) for up to "six months prior" to the time when the person was approved for Medicaid.

Let's suppose we have a married couple (traditionally, <u>intentional gifting does not apply</u> in a married case and transfers between spouses are exempt), and the husband enters a nursing home on February 1, 2017. It's now June 13, 2017. The couple has $300,000 in assets. The Community Spouse/Wife keeps $120,900 as her CSRA, and the Institutionalized Spouse/Husband can keep $8,000 (assuming his income meets that test), leaving $171,100 to buy a qualified annuity for the wife. One of the spouses could ask that the husband's income be directed first to the payment of the nursing home bill for the period between February 1 and June 13, leaving more income through the annuity for the wife. (Note: if the Institutional Spouse dies before the balance is paid off, then the Community Spouse is responsible for the payment.)

ASSETS ACQUIRED AFTER MEDICAID APPROVAL

1. Suppose Mary inherits $100,000. This has no effect on the eligibility of her husband, John, who can stay in the nursing home as long as she retains sole ownership of the funds.

2. Suppose that John is in the nursing home and inherits $100,000 after he was approved for Medicaid, but while paying for the nursing home privately during a penalty period. He could spend down the money on home repairs, replenish the CSRA, or use the funds to pay care costs at the nursing home instead of tapping other resources.

3. If John still owns some of the funds he inherited in the previous situation, or if he comes into funds after a penalty period has expired and he is receiving Medicaid benefits, he could transfer the funds to Mary. Since that transfer is to a spouse, it is exempt, and then she could purchase a Medicaid Compliant Annuity.

4. Each year, the Medicaid rules require that the applicant in the nursing home recertify that he (or she) is still eligible for benefits.

PRE-PLANNING OPTIONS TO PAY FOR LONG TERM CARE AND TO PROTECT ASSETS

The Irrevocable Trust

Currently, Medicaid guidelines permit the government to look back for a period of five years from the date of application for uncompensated transfers, which creates a period of ineligibility. This time period was increased from three years under the Deficit Reduction Act of 2005. If you are in good health and unlikely to need long-term care services, one asset protection strategy would be to transfer that which you wish to protect into an Irrevocable Trust. Many people who are unfamiliar with the workings of this type of instrument will initially shy away from its use. However, once they have more information, they see it as a tremendous vehicle to protect their assets from creditors, predators, and the costs associated with long-term care.

The creators of these trusts, also referred to as the Settlors, can retain many controls over the assets deposited. These controls include, for example, the ability to gain income from the assets, to change the beneficiaries, continued use of the property as their principal residence, the capital gains exclusion, and the achievement step up in tax basis at death on their home.

While it is generally not a good idea to transfer all of your assets into an Irrevocable Trust, it is often a very useful tool to protect a substantial portion of your estate from the catastrophic costs of long-term care.

Long Term Care Insurance with Hybrid Policies

Stand-alone long-term care policies are rapidly disappearing. Many companies have ceased offering the product, while those who have not stopped have greatly increased premiums. Additionally, the underwriting guidelines for qualification have become increasingly difficult.

A new type of product has largely stepped in to fill the void and consumers' needs. These are hybrid policies with linked benefits. In the past, consumers were less inclined to buy long-term care policies because if they never had the need to use them for long-term care, they received no other benefit from the policy. Today, these policies come with cash value which can be accessed: a death benefit if you don't need the funds during life and a long-term care component to draw from as a type of advance of the death benefit. These policies can be individually structured to change the amount of monthly benefit you receive, the length of time you would receive the benefit, the manner of the premium payment (annual or lump sum), and the elimination period (similar to a deductible).

Also, it is typically easier to qualify for these products.

Finally, hybrid products are attractive because, under certain conditions, clients can convert existing products or policies—including life insurance, annuities, and other similar products or policies—into a new similar policy with the additional long-term care benefit through IRS regulations, i.e. a 1035 exchange.

Disability Income Insurance

This book has focused on ways to pay for long-term care expenses and protect your assets you have managed to save. However, the basis for almost all estate planning is the income used to fund the plan. If you are still in your working years, disability income insurance is an invaluable piece of your estate planning. The costs of long-term care aside, should you become disabled during the course of your working career, your income may either be greatly reduced or abruptly come to an end.

Many individuals have not "insured" their income at all, or they are under the mistaken impression that they have adequate coverage. Short-term disability benefits are typically meager at best, while long-term benefits rarely provide enough coverage to permit individuals to maintain their accustomed standard of living. Furthermore, if you do have coverage and separate from your employer, as you get older, this coverage becomes much more expensive to obtain, if not impossible.

Before you have a life event which can greatly drive up the cost of coverage, if not totally prevent the option, you should seek out the advice of a qualified Disability Income Insurance agent to assess your need and the cost of such coverage.

www.ingramcontent.com/pod-product-compliance
Lightning Source LLC
Chambersburg PA
CBHW050014230526
45470CB00003B/954